AF539152

SUNNY
SIDE UP

Published 2026

FiNGERPRINT!

Prakash Books

Fingerprint Publishing

@FingerprintP

@fingerprintpublishingbooks

www.fingerprintpublishing.com

ISBN: 978 93 5856 846 2

To ....
From ....

Radiant souls embrace the sunny side of life.

In a world where our lives are often overshadowed by storm clouds of doubt and negativity, there exists a remarkable light that shines through these dark moments—your sunshine.

Being your own sunshine means cultivating self-love, self-acceptance, and a positive mindset. Embrace the fact that you have the key to your own happiness.

When your inner radiance shines through, grab your sunglasses, because

WE ARE DOING LIFE SUNNY SIDE UP!

“HUMOR IS
THE SUNSHINE
OF THE MIND.”

EDWARD BULWER
LYTTON

"Don't let the shadows
of yesterday spoil the
sunshine of tomorrow
Live for today."

NANDINA MORRIS

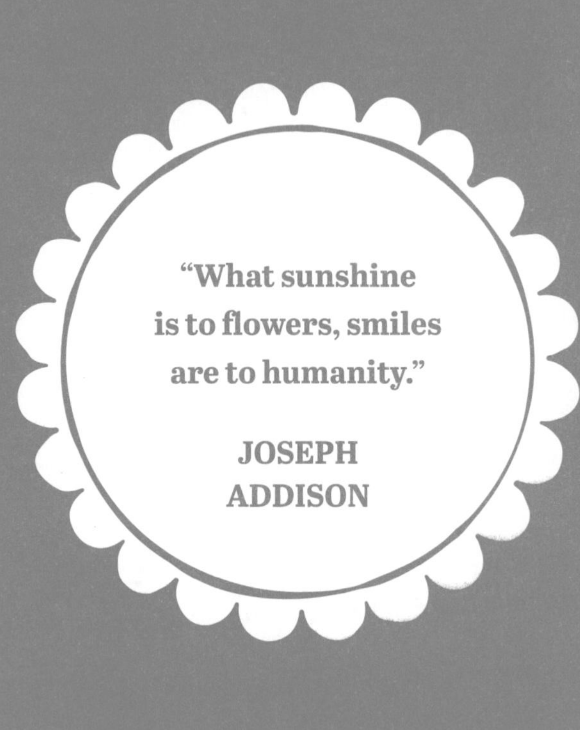
"What sunshine
is to flowers, smiles
are to humanity."
JOSEPH
ADDISON

"It's the artist's business
to create sunshine
when the sun falls."
ROMAIN
ROLLAND

“A GOOD LAUGH IS SUNSHINE IN THE HOUSE.”

William Makepeace Thackeray

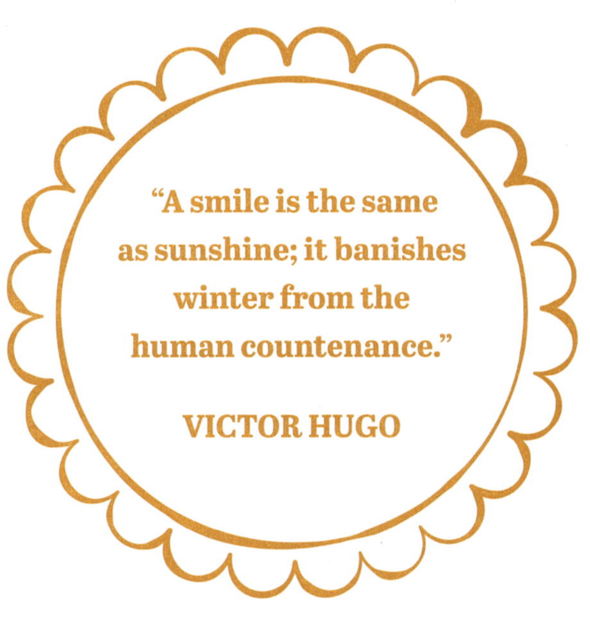
"A smile is the same
as sunshine; it banishes
winter from the
human countenance."
VICTOR HUGO

"Keep your face always
towards the sunshine
and shadows will
fall behind you."

WALT WHITMAN

"Sunshine is delicious,
rain is refreshing,
wind braces us up, snow
is exhilarating; there
is really no such thing as
bad weather, only different
kinds of good weather."

JOHN RUSKIN

"And so with the sunshine
and the great bursts of leaves
growing on the trees, just
as things grow in fast movies
I had that familiar conviction
that life was beginning
over again with the summer."

F. SCOTT FITZGERALD

"IF YOU WANT TO
SHINE LIKE A SUN,
FIRST BURN LIKE A SUN."

A. P. J. Abdul Kalam

"SOME DAYS YOU HAVE TO CREATE YOUR OWN SUNSHINE."

SAM SUNDQUIST

“Don’t be pushed around
by the fears in your mind.
Be led by the dreams
in your heart.”

ROY T. BENNETT

**"LIVE IN THE SUNSHINE,
SWIM THE SEA,
DRINK THE WILD AIR."**

Ralph Waldo Emerson

“THINK OF THE DAY ALIVE WITH SUNSHINE, NOT THE DISMAL DAYS OF RAIN.”

Robert E. Farley

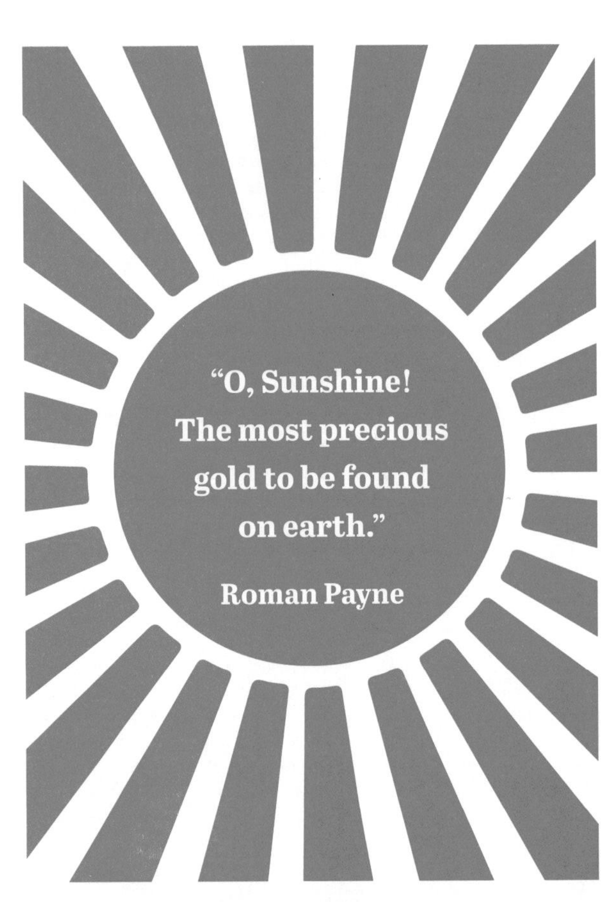
"O, Sunshine!
The most precious
gold to be found
on earth."
Roman Payne

**“JUST LIVING IS NOT ENOUGH . . .
ONE MUST HAVE SUNSHINE,
FREEDOM, AND A LITTLE FLOWER.”**

HANS CHRISTIAN ANDERSEN

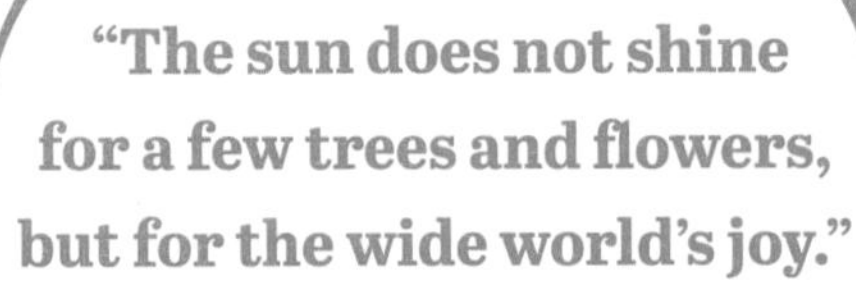

HENRY
WARD BEECHER

"Far away there in the sunshine are my highest aspirations. I may not reach them, but I can look up and see their beauty, believe in them, and try to follow where they lead."

LOUISA MAY ALCOTT

"SOME OLD FASHIONED THINGS LIKE FRESH AIR AND SUNSHINE ARE HARD TO BEAT."

Laura Ingalls Wilder

"WHEN YOU COME TO THE END OF YOUR ROPE, TIE A KNOT AND HANG ON."

FRANKLIN D. ROOSEVELT

"Today, give a stranger
one of your smiles.
It might be the
only sunshine
he sees all day."

H. JACKSON BROWN

"The sun is a daily reminder that we too can rise again from the darkness, that we too can shine our own light."

S. AJNA

"A COMPLIMENT IS VERBAL SUNSHINE."

ROBERT ORBEN

"LOOK AT THE SUNNY SIDE OF EVERYTHING."

CHRISTIAN D. LARSEN

"The greatest glory in living lies not in never falling, but in rising every time we fall."

NELSON MANDELA

"Anything is possible
with sunshine
and a little pink."
Lilly Pultizer

"NO MATTER HOW HARD THE PAST, YOU CAN ALWAYS BEGIN AGAIN."

BUDDHA

"HE THAT WILL ENJOY THE BRIGHTNESS OF SUNSHINE, MUST QUIT THE COOLNESS OF THE SHADE."

SAMUEL JOHNSON

“LIFE ISN’T ABOUT WAITING FOR THE STORM TO PASS, IT’S ABOUT LEARNING HOW TO DANCE IN THE RAIN.”

Vivian Greene

"Nobody needs a smile so much as the one who has none to give. So get used to smiling heart—warming smiles, and you will spread sunshine in a sometimes dreary world."

LAWRENCE G. LOVASIK

“WHEN THE GOING GETS TOUGH,
THE TOUGH GET GOING.”

JOSEPH P. KENNEDY

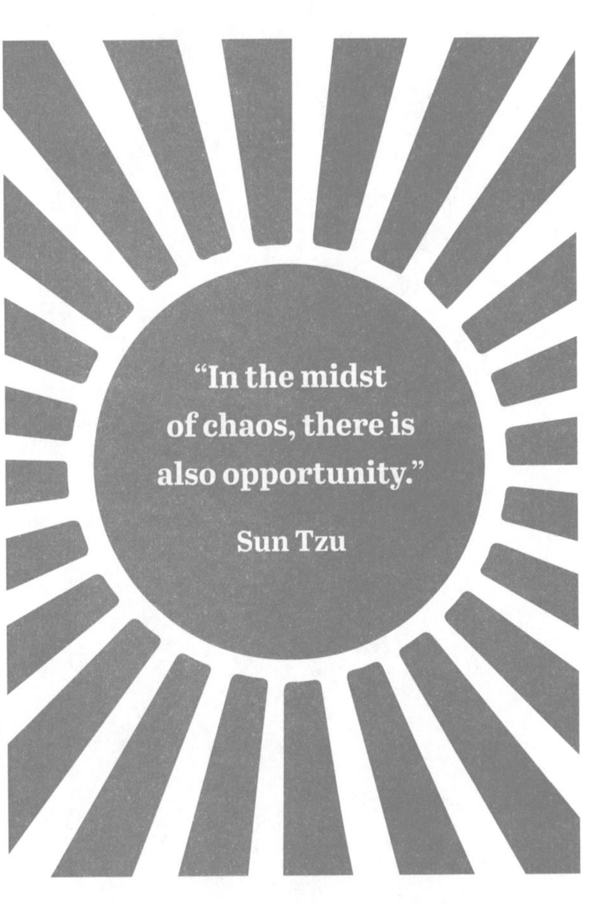
"In the midst
of chaos, there is
also opportunity."
Sun Tzu

"God gives us the sunshine of hope everyday. It's up to us to find and bask in it daily."

TIMOTHY PINA

"THE PESSIMIST COMPLAINS ABOUT THE WIND; THE OPTIMIST EXPECTS IT TO CHANGE; THE REALIST ADJUSTS THE SAILS."

WILLIAM ARTHUR WARD

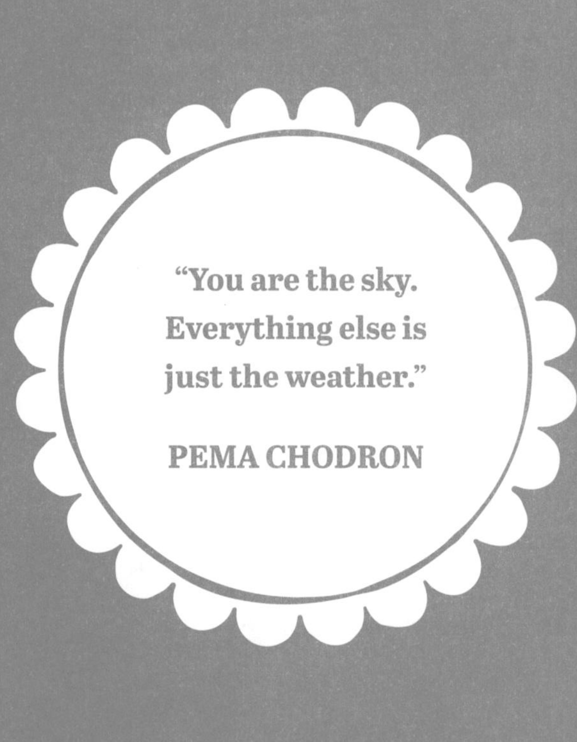
"You are the sky.
Everything else is
just the weather."
PEMA CHODRON

"When you can't change the direction of the wind, adjust your sails."

H. JACKSON BROWN JR.

"TRY TO BE A RAINBOW IN SOMEONE'S CLOUD."

MAYA ANGELOU

"BE SOMEONE'S SUNSHINE WHEN THEIR SKIES ARE GREY."

ANONYMOUS

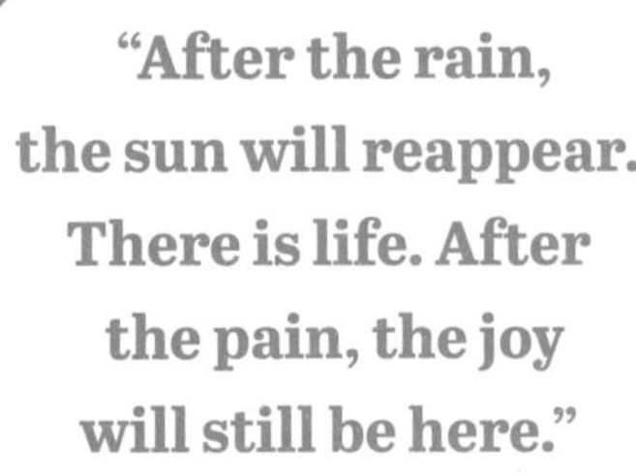
"After the rain,
the sun will reappear.
There is life. After
the pain, the joy
will still be here."
WALT DISNEY

“Surround yourself with people who make you laugh. Laughter is to the soul what sunshine is to a flower.”

PEGGY TONEY HORTON

“LAUGHTER IS MAGIC THAT DISPENSES CLOUDS AND CREATES SUNSHINE IN THE SOUL.”

Richelle E. Goodrich

"In your darkest hour, give thanks, for in due time, the morning will come. And it will come with a ray of sunshine."

MICHAEL BASSEY JOHNSON

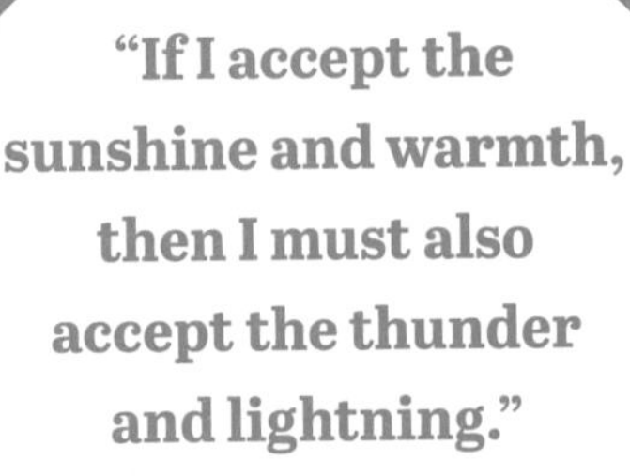

KHALIL GIBRAN

"MAY YOU SEE SUNSHINE WHERE OTHERS SEE SHADOWS AND OPPORTUNITIES WHERE OTHERS SEE OBSTACLES."

ANONYMOUS

"THE EARTH WOULD DIE IF THE SUN STOPPED KISSING HER."

Hafez

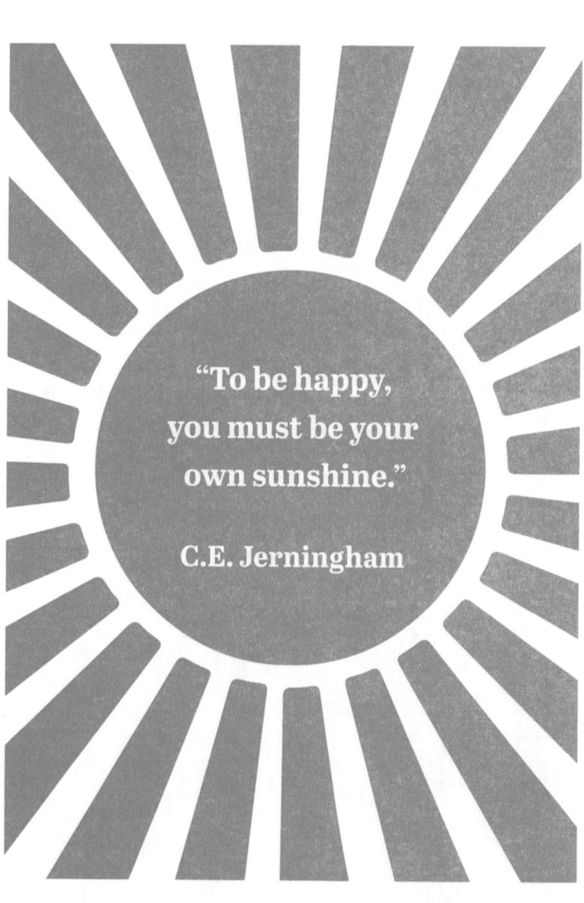
"To be happy,
you must be your
own sunshine."
C.E. Jerningham

“EVERY MORNING BRINGS NEW POTENTIAL, BUT ONLY IF YOU MAKE THE MOST OF IT.”

HARVEY MACKAY

"WE MUST ACCEPT FINITE DISAPPOINTMENT, BUT NEVER LOSE INFINITE HOPE."

MARTIN LUTHER KING JR.

"Smile, though your heart
is aching smile, even though
it's breaking, when there are
clouds in the sky, you'll get by
If you smile through your pain
and sorrow. Smile and maybe
tomorrow, you'll see the sun
come shining through for you."

CHARLIE CHAPLIN

"THE HARDER THE CONFLICT,
THE GREATER THE TRIUMPH."

GEORGE WASHINGTON

CELEBRATE YOUR UNIQUENESS!

Just like the sun, you are one of a kind.

Embrace your quirks, talents, and imperfections, and watch how your light brightens the world.

Stand out in the crowd and radiate your own brand of sunshine.

While some may still be in the rain, choose to spread kindness like confetti and believe that your light has the power to create a ripple effect of positivity.

So, go ahead, sunshine!

Keep shining like a magnificent soul.

"If you realized how powerful your thoughts are, you would never think a negative thought."

Peace Pilgrim

"You are never too old to
set another goal or to
dream a new dream."

C.S. LEWIS

"SOME PEOPLE ARE
SO MUCH SUNSHINE
TO THE SQUARE INCH."

WALT WHITMAN

“A SUNNY DISPOSITION IS WORTH MORE THAN A FORTUNE.”

ANDREW CARNEGIE

"WITHOUT STORMY DAYS, WE FORGET TO VALUE SUNNY SKIES."

Cathy Burnham Martin

“MAY SUNSHINE SURROUND YOU EACH NEW DAY. AND MAY SMILES AND LOVE NEVER BE FAR AWAY.”

CATHERINE PULSIFER

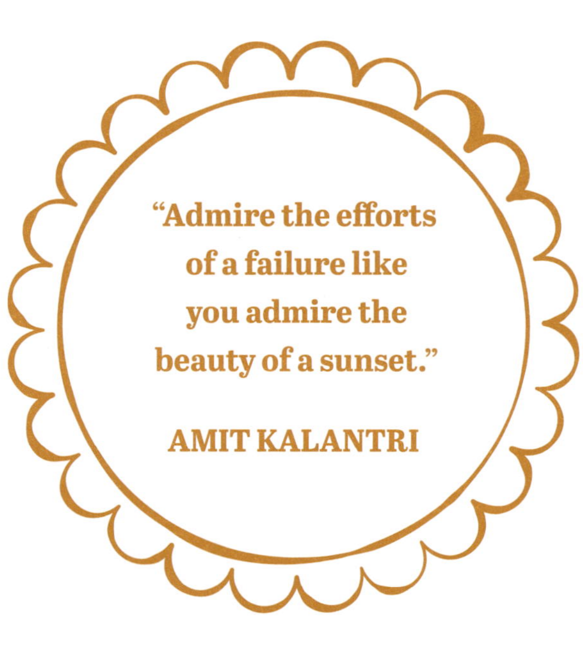
"Admire the efforts
of a failure like
you admire the
beauty of a sunset."
AMIT KALANTRI

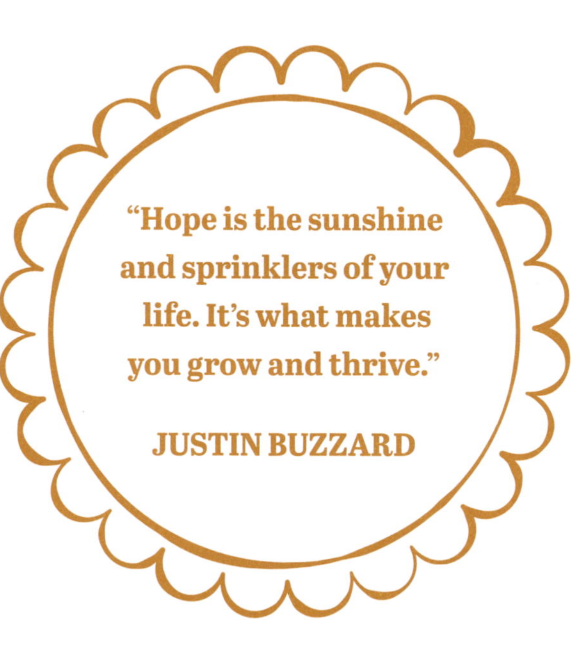
“Hope is the sunshine
and sprinklers of your
life. It’s what makes
you grow and thrive.”
JUSTIN BUZZARD

"To say goodbye,
is to die a little.
To say good morning,
is a hope for a
new sunshine in
a cloudy winter."

NABIL TOUSSI

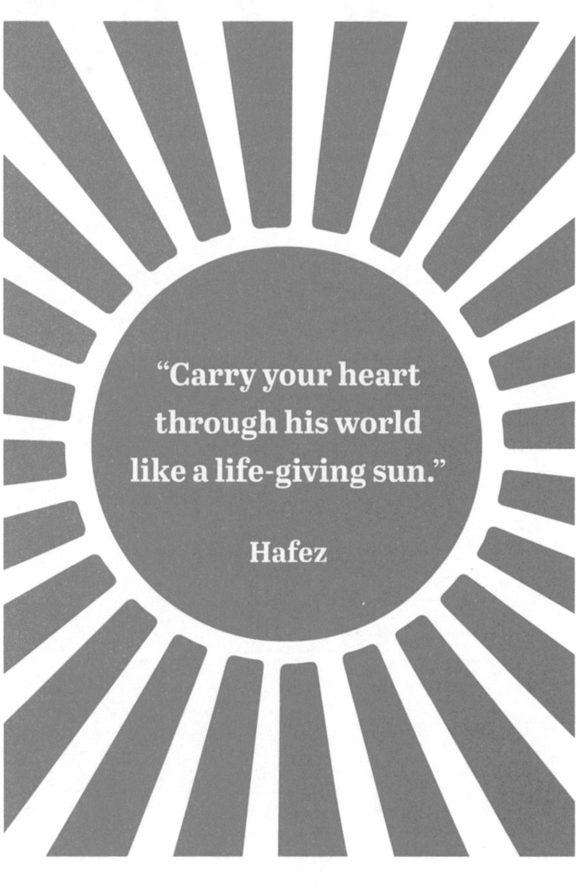
"Carry your heart
through his world
like a life-giving sun."
Hafez

"Your days are numbered.
Use them to throw open
the windows of your soul
to the sun. If you do not,
the sun will soon set,
and you with it."

MARCUS AURELIUS

"Hope is like the sun,
which, as we journey toward
it, casts the shadow of our
burden behind us."

SAMUEL SMILES

“EVEN DIRT GLITTERS WHEN THE SUN IS SHINING UPON IT.”

JOHANN WOLFGANG VON GOETHE

"Concentrate all your thoughts upon the work at hand. The sun's rays do not burn until brought to a focus."

ALEXANDER GRAHAM BELL

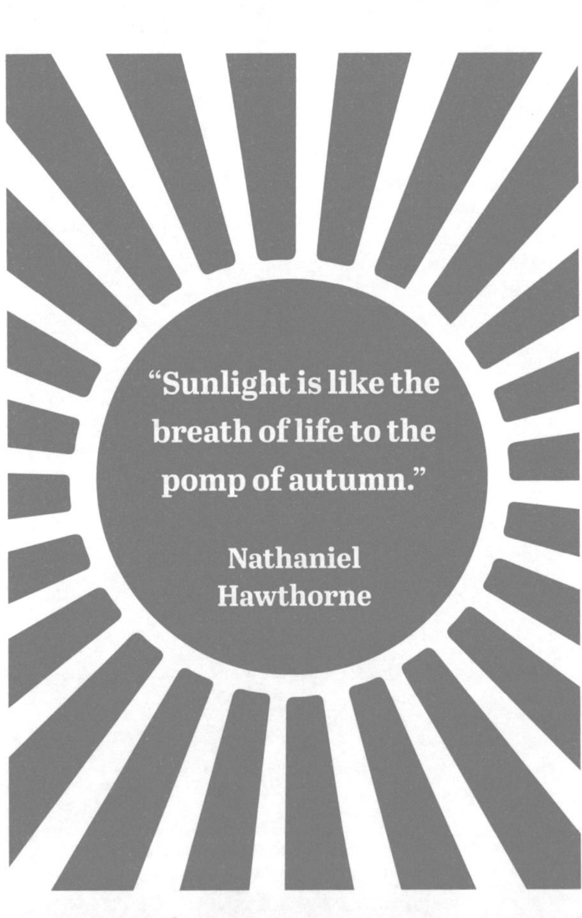
"Sunlight is like the breath of life to the pomp of autumn."
Nathaniel Hawthorne

“THE TIME TO REPAIR THE ROOF IS WHEN THE SUN IS SHINING.”

John F. Kennedy

“IF YOU WANT TO FEEL THE SUNSHINE, CHANGE POSITION!”

ERNEST AGYEMANG YEBOAH

"LET THERE BE SUNSHINE IN YOUR SOUL TODAY!"

ANONYMOUS

"Compliment people
wherever you go.
Praise every single
thing you see.
Be a ray of sunshine
to everyone you meet."

RHONDA BYRNE

"I used to cover my windows in heavy curtains, never drawn. Now I danced in the sunlight on my hardwood floors."

KIMBERLY NOVOSEL

"Don't bring me
the stars from the sky,
I'm planting sunshine
in my backyard."

Sanhita
Baruah

"Don't wait for someone
to bring you flowers.
Plant your own garden and
decorate your own soul."

MARIO QUINTANA

“LAUGHTER IS A SUNBEAM OF THE SOUL.”

THOMAS MANN

"Behind every dark cloud there is an ever-shining sun. Just wait. In time, the cloud will pass."

MARIANNE WILLIAMSON

"After every storm the sun will smile; for every problem there is a solution, and the soul's indefeasible duty is to be of good cheer."

WILLIAM ROUNSEVILLE ALGER

"WHY NOT SEE WHICH IS BRIGHTER: YOUR AURA OR THE SUN?"

Richelle Mead

"THOU ART THE SUN
OF OTHER DAYS.
THEY SHINE BY GIVING
BACK THE RAYS."

JOHN KEBLE

"I WAS RICH,
IF NOT IN MONEY,
IN SUNNY HOURS
AND SUMMER DAYS . . ."

HENRY DAVID THOREAU

"The real you is loving, joyful, and free. The real you is just like a flower, just like the wind, just like the ocean, just like the sun."

DON MIGUEL RUIZ

"ANOTHER SUNRISE,
ANOTHER NEW BEGINNING."

JONATHAN LOCKWOOD HUIE

"Learn from flowers—always angle towards the sun."
Maureen Joyce Connolly

"EVERY FLOWER IS A SOUL BLOSSOMING IN NATURE."

Gérard De Nerval

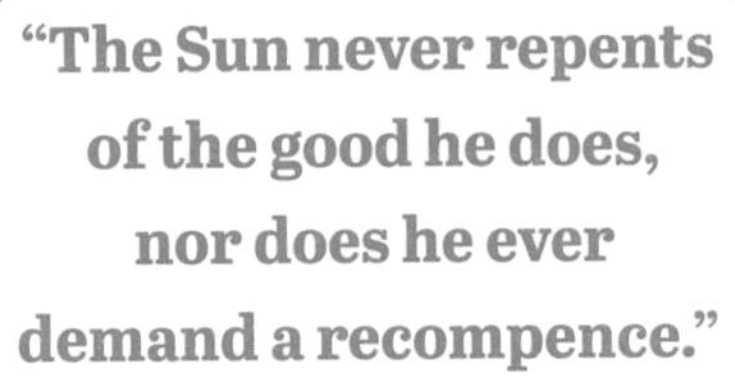

"The Sun never repents of the good he does, nor does he ever demand a recompence."

BENJAMIN FRANKLIN

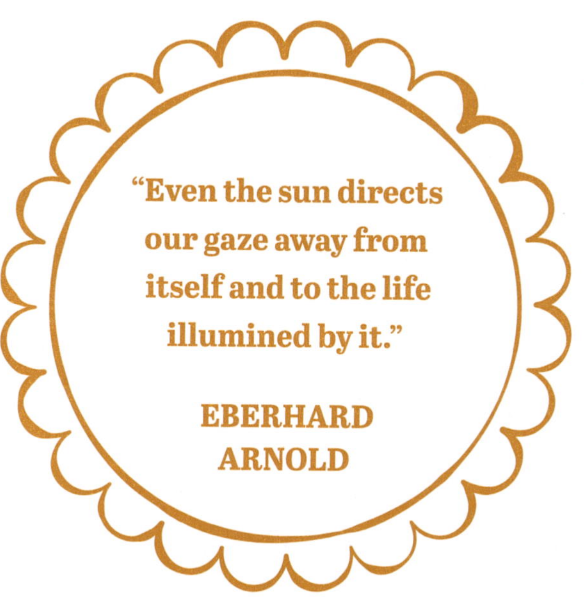
"Even the sun directs our gaze away from itself and to the life illumined by it."
EBERHARD ARNOLD

"THE SUN SHINES UPON GOOD AND BAD ALIKE."

HANS CHRISTIAN ANDERSEN

"Birds sing after a storm;
why shouldn't people feel
as free to delight in whatever
sunlight remains to them?"

ROSE KENNEDY

"BE LIKE THE SUN AND MEADOW, WHICH ARE NOT IN THE LEAST CONCERNED ABOUT THE COMING WINTER."

GEORGE BERNARD SHAW

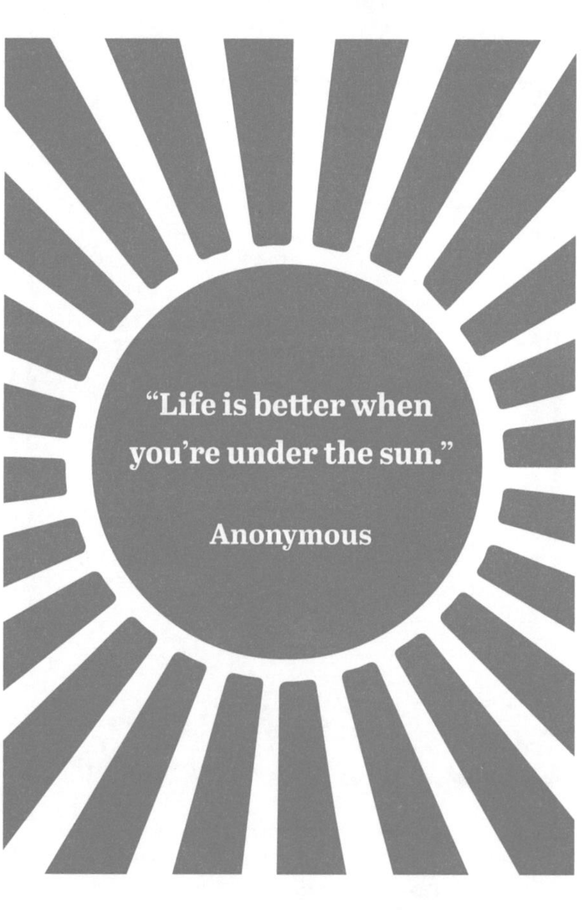
“Life is better when
you’re under the sun.”
Anonymous

"The Sun himself is weak
when he first rises and
gathers strength and
courage as the day gets on."

CHARLES DICKENS

"THE LOW SUN STARES THROUGH DUST OF GOLD."

Alexander Smith

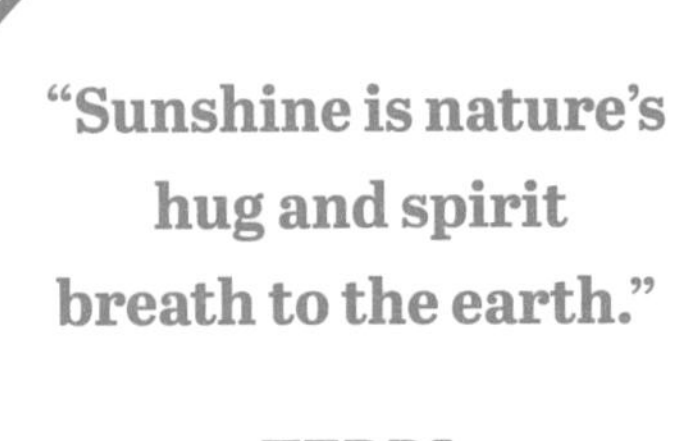

"Sunshine is nature's hug and spirit breath to the earth."

TERRI GUILLEMETS

"The Sun can be your
greatest gloom, or
your greatest comforter,
depending on how
you view its shine."

ANTHONY LICCIONE

"IT NEVER HURTS TO KEEP LOOKING FOR SUNSHINE."

A. A. Milne

"The greatest pleasure in life is doing what people say you cannot do."

WALTER BAGEHOT

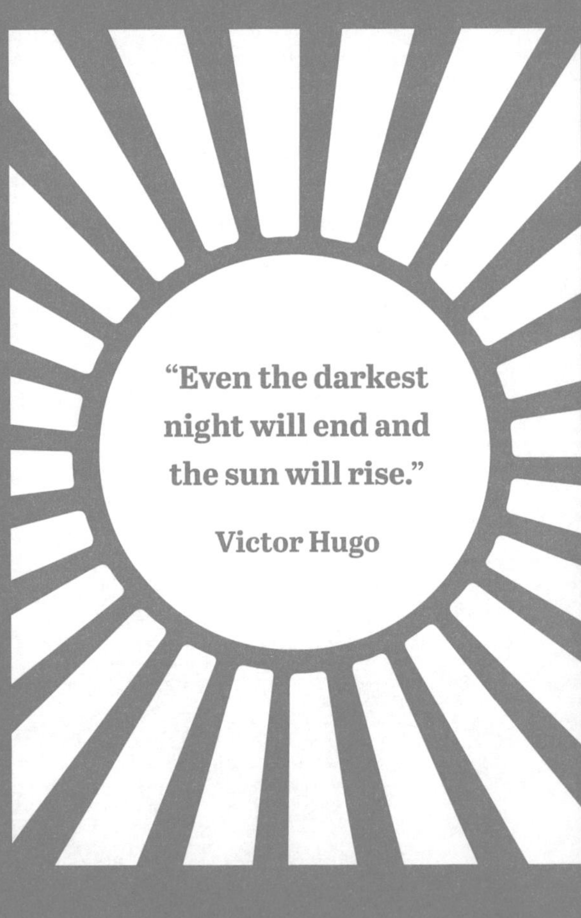
"Even the darkest
night will end and
the sun will rise."
Victor Hugo

"THE SUN IS SHINING AND SO SHALL YOU."

TONI ALEO

“SUNSHINE WILL GUIDE YOUR HEART EVEN IN THE DARKEST OF DAYS.”

ANTHONY T. HINCKS

"I'D RATHER CHASE THE SUN THAN WAIT FOR IT."

Markus Zusak

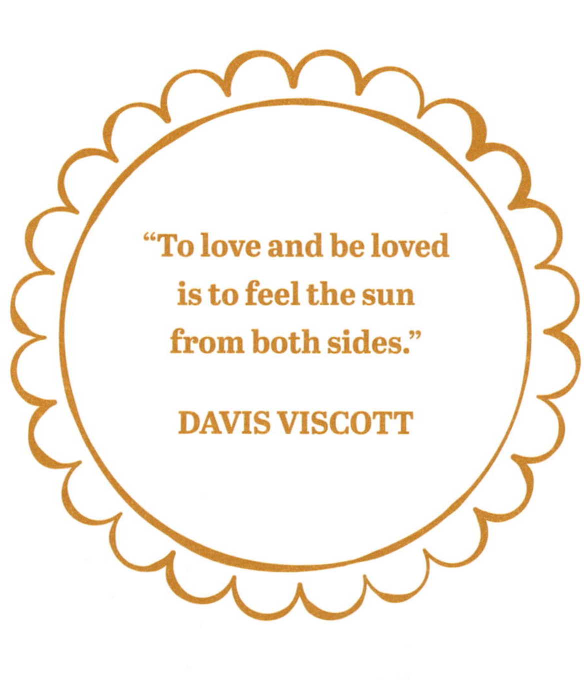
"To love and be loved
is to feel the sun
from both sides."
DAVIS VISCOTT

"LOVE COMFORTETH LIKE SUNSHINE AFTER RAIN."

WILLIAM SHAKESPEARE

"MOST OF THE SHADOWS OF THIS LIFE ARE CAUSED BY STANDING IN ONE'S OWN SUNSHINE."

Ralph Waldo Emerson

"Some people are making such thorough preparation for rainy days that they aren't enjoying today's sunshine."

WILLIAM FEATHER

"None appreciates rainbow
and sunshine better
than he on whos
parade it has rained."

VINCENT OKAY NWACHUKWU

**"IN EVERY PERSON
THERE IS A SUN.
JUST LET THEM SHINE."**

Socrates

"HEALTH AND GOOD HUMOR ARE TO THE HUMAN BODY LIKE SUNSHINE TO VEGETATION."

JEAN B. MASSILLON

"WHO ATE YOUR BOWL OF SUNSHINE THIS MORNING, THUNDERCLOUD?"

ANONYMOUS

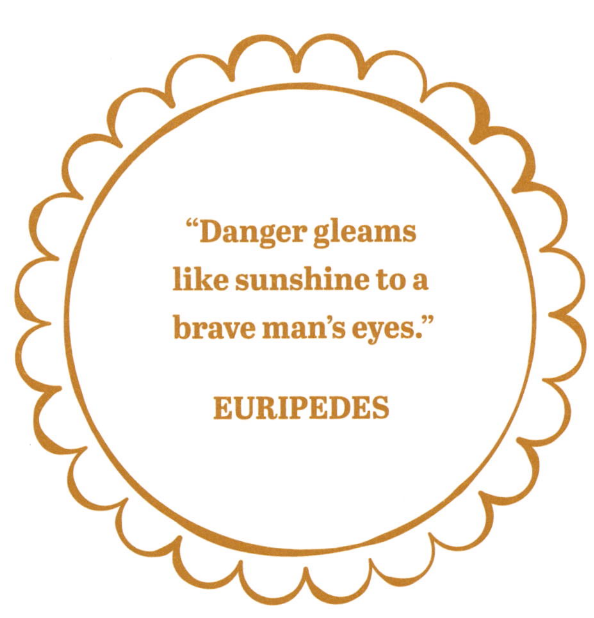

"Danger gleams like sunshine to a brave man's eyes."

EURIPEDES

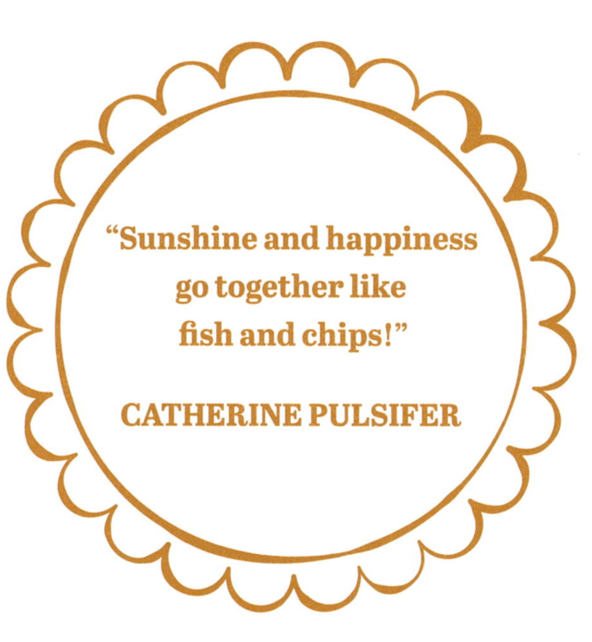
"Sunshine and happiness
go together like
fish and chips!"
CATHERINE PULSIFER

"EVEN WHEN IT'S RAINING, THE SUNSHINE IS STILL THERE."

CLARE JOSA

"I've found that there is always some beauty left—in nature, sunshine, freedom—in yourself; these can all help you."

ANNE FRANK

“THERE ARE ALWAYS FLOWERS FOR THOSE WHO WANT TO SEE THEM.”

HENRI MATISSE

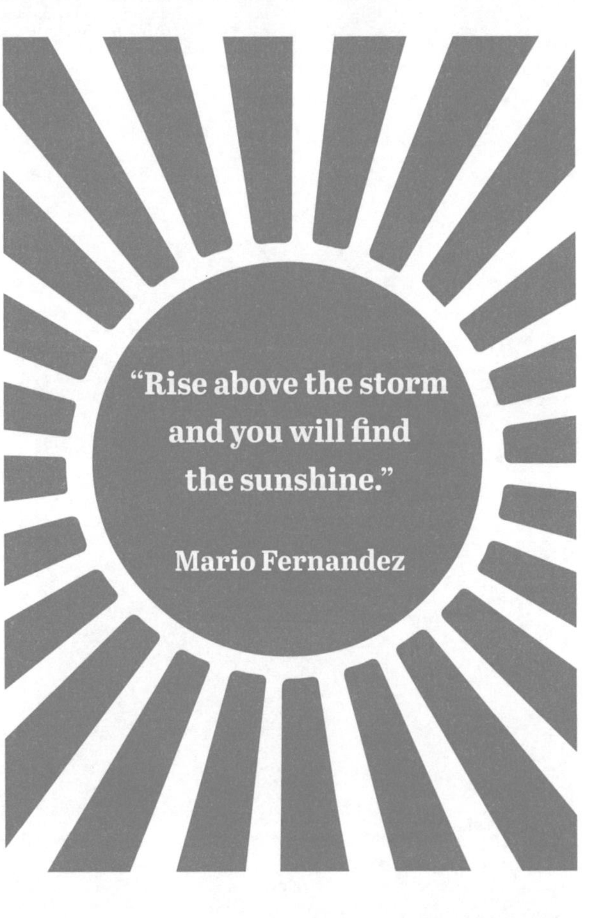

“Rise above the storm
and you will find
the sunshine.”
Mario Fernandez

"When the sun is shining
I can do anything;
no mountain is too
high, no trouble too
difficult to overcome."

WILMA RUDOLPH

"LAUGHTER IS THE SUN
THAT DRIVES WINTER
FROM THE HUMAN FACE."

Victor Hugo

"Don't confuse your path with your destination. Just because it's stormy now, doesn't mean you aren't headed for sunshine."

DR. ANTHONY FERNANDO

"Shadows can indicate
what's shining bright.
But it's the sun which
fills your soul with light."

RUMI

"Watch the sun until it comes into your body and stays as a tiny sun. It will keep your face shining even in the coldest of winter."

YOKO ONO

"HOW LOVELY YELLOW IS!
IT STANDS FOR THE SUN."

VINCENT VAN GOGH

"Difficulties are meant to rouse, not discourage. The human spirit is to grow strong by conflict."

WILLIAM ELLERY CHANNING

"IT IS ETERNITY NOW.
I AM IN THE MIDST OF IT.
IT IS ABOUT ME
AND THE SUNSHINE."

RICHARD JEFFERIES

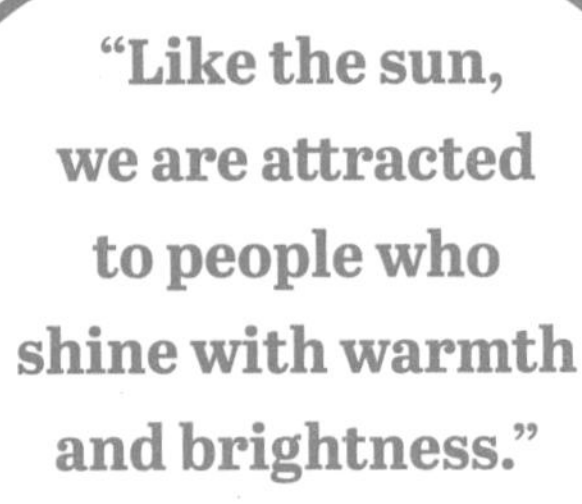

"Like the sun,
we are attracted
to people who
shine with warmth
and brightness."

**ANTHONY D.
WILLIAMS**

"You either live
under a rock or you
walk in the sunshine.
That's pretty much
how it goes."

SIXTO RODRIGUEZ

"The Sun. The bright Sun,
that brings back, not
light alone, but new life,
and hope, and freshness
to manburst upon the
crowded city in clear
and radiant glory."

CHARLES DICKENS

"I'M 100 PERCENT SUNSHINE."

LIL YACHTY

"Don't wait for someone
else to bring you flowers.
Plant your own garden
and decorate your own soul."

LUTHER BURBANK

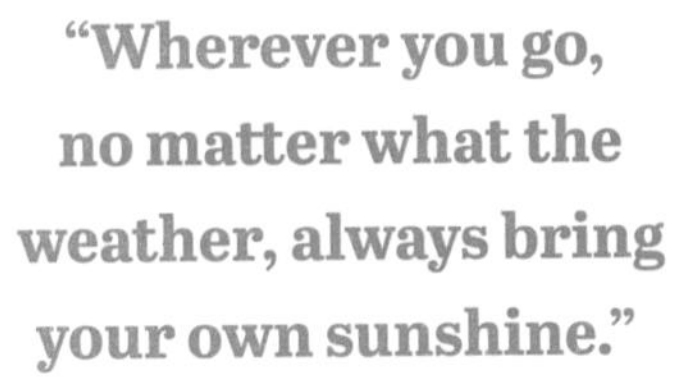

"Wherever you go,
no matter what the
weather, always bring
your own sunshine."

**ANTHONY J.
D'ANGELO**

"IF YOU DANCE LIKE RAINDROPS,THERE WILL ALWAYS BE SUNSHINE."

CURTIS TYRONE JONES

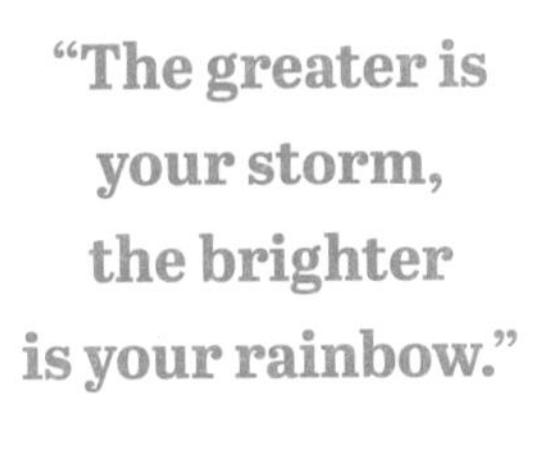
"The greater is
your storm,
the brighter
is your rainbow."
Anonymous

"Remember even though the outside world might be raining, if you keep on smiling the sun will soon show its face and smile back at you."

ANNA LEE

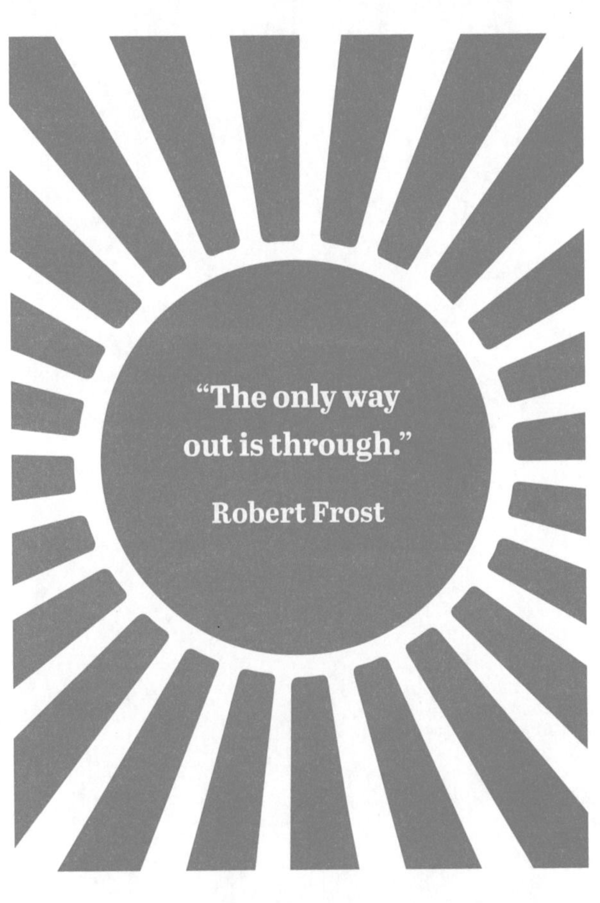
"The only way
out is through."
Robert Frost

"Part of being optimistic
is keeping one's head
pointed toward the sun,
one's feet moving forward."

NELSON MANDELA

"I BELIEVE IN
THE SUN, EVEN
WHEN IT RAINS."

Anne Frank

"EVEN FOR ME LIFE HAD ITS GLEAMS OF SUNSHINE."

CHARLOTTE BRONTE

“REMEMBER, YOU’RE THE ONE WHO CAN FILL THE WORLD WITH SUNSHINE.”

"It's always sunny
above the clouds.
Always. Every day
on earth—every day
I have ever had—was
secretly sunny, after all."

CAITLIN MORAN

“THE DARKNESS IS AT ITS DEEPEST JUST BEFORE THE SUNRISE.”

VOLTAIRE

“THE SUN IS ALONE TOO BUT IT STILL SHINES.”

ANONYMOUS

"IF YOU WANT TO SEE THE SUNSHINE, YOU HAVE TO WEATHER THE STORM."

FRANK LANE

"THE SUN STILL SHINES, EVEN WHEN IT'S HIDING."

A. A. Milne

"Let there always be a bright spot in your heart for the people around you. They might need a bit of sunshine."

RON BARATONO

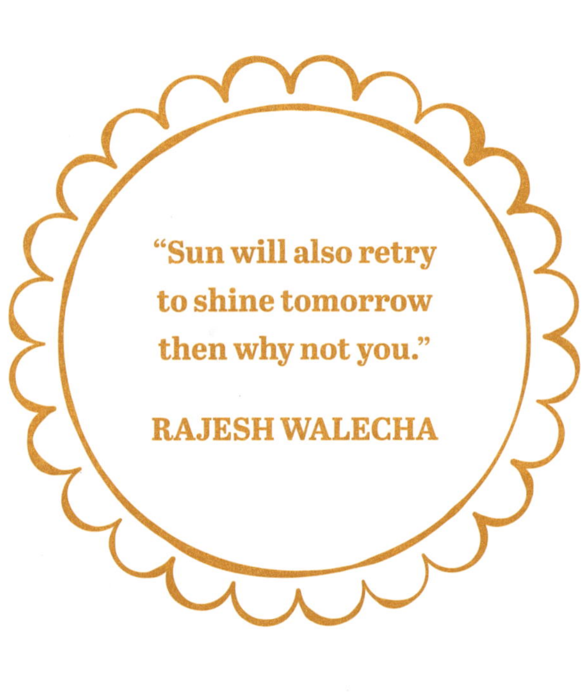
"Sun will also retry
to shine tomorrow
then why not you."
RAJESH WALECHA

"EVERY ADVERSITY, EVERY FAILURE, EVERY HEARTACHE CARRIES WITH IT THE SEED OF AN EQUAL OR GREATER BENEFIT."

NAPOLEON HILL

"HAVE A RAY OF SUNSHINE AND LIGHT WITH YOU EVERYWHERE YOU MAY GO."

LAILAH GIFTY AKITA

"Through the portals
of silence, the healing sun
of wisdom and peace
will shine upon you."

**PARAMAHANSA
YOGANANDA**

“WHY SHOULD WE GROPE AMONG THE DRY BONES OF THE PAST? THE SUN SHINES TODAY ALSO.”

Ralph Waldo Emerson

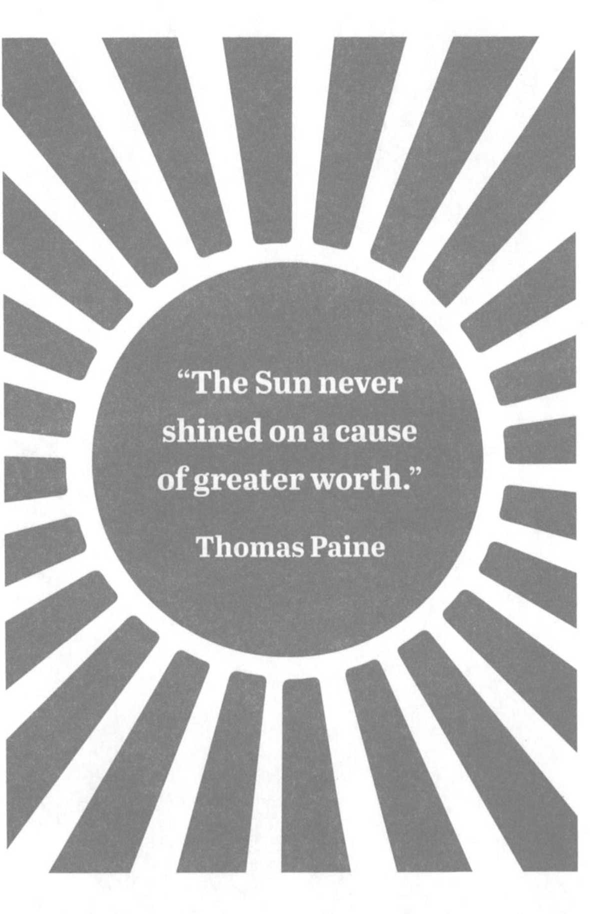
"The Sun never
shined on a cause
of greater worth."
Thomas Paine

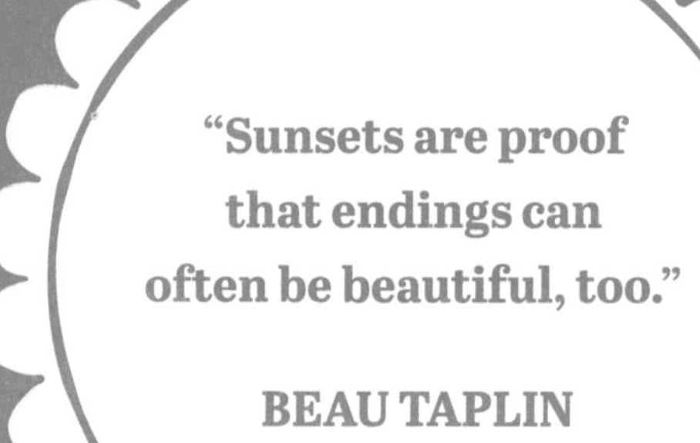
"Sunsets are proof
that endings can
often be beautiful, too."
BEAU TAPLIN

"Faith is the virtue of the storm, just as the happiness is the virtue of sunshine."

RUTH FULTON BENEDICT

“MAKE HAY WHILE THE SUN SHINES.”

Miguel de Cervantes